Let's pretend

Story by Annette Smith
Illustrations by Naomi C. Lewis

2

Look at Emma.

Emma is a bear.

Emma is happy.

4

Look at Matthew.

Matthew is a rabbit.

Matthew is not happy.

"Grr-grr!" said Emma.

"I am a bear.

I am a **big** bear!

Grr-grr!"

tiger

"Mom!" said Matthew.

"Look at my book.

Look at the **tiger**!"

"Here is the tiger's nose,"

said Mom.

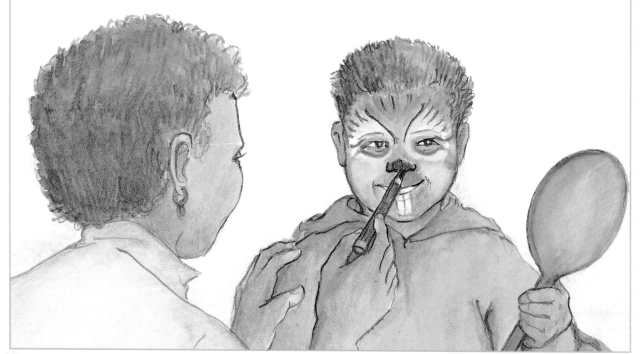

10

"Here is the tiger's mouth."

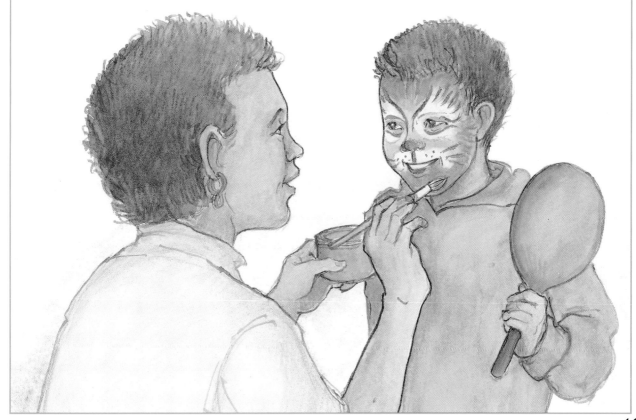

"And here is a tail

for Matthew the tiger,"

said Mom.

"Grr-grr!" said Matthew.

"I am a tiger.

I am a **big** tiger.

Grr-grr!"

Look at Matthew and Emma.